Essential
of entrepreneurship

ANA MARIA FLORENTINA

Copyright © 2024 Author Name

All rights reserved.

ISBN: 9798333029430

DEDICATION

This book is dedicated to those who want to accumulate knowledge in entrepreneurship, so they can capitalize on useful information of great authors in economics, as well as personal opinions. Entrepreneurship is based on innovation and the big problem at the moment is the lack of it. Peter Duker says "wherever you work you can change the way you do things and that change could have huge effects" and the effects will be seen in national economies.

CONTENTS

	Acknowledgments	i
1	Chapter Aspects of entrepreneurship and the entrepreneur	1
2	Chapter Characteristics of the entrepreneur	3
3	Chapter The risks for an entrepreneur	5
4	Chapter Entrepreneurial strategies	7
5	Chapter Stimulating entrepreneurship	8
6	Chapter Involvement of timers in entrepreneurship activities	10
7	Chapter Problems faced by entrepreneurship	13
8	Chapter Solutions related to the problems analyzed in the previous chapter	15

ACKNOWLEDGMENTS

I would like to thank those who are attentive to this information, which I find useful in running a business as well as starting one.

1 CHAPTER ASPECTS OF ENTREPRENEURSHIP AND THE ENTREPRENEUR

Often economic growth is due to the development and implementation of new ideas, and surprising is the ignorant way in which economics has treated entrepreneurship. It has not been neglected from a critical perspective, but from an analytical one. If we look into the context of the past, we can certainly notice that there was no terminology of the word "entrepreneur". Often terms such as "adventurers" or "producers" were claimed to it. It was Schumpeter who theorized the concept, but in essence the French economist Richard Cantillon, the French economist Richard Cantillon, was the originator of the term "entrepreneur" (meaning "to undertake something").

The dimensions of glory, fame and wealth carry significant importance, even if they often do not materialize. That's why "for the entrepreneur, completing an imagined success is only part of the material reward". If we look at things chronologically, a first approach to entrepreneurship has its roots in Joseph Schumpeter's Capitalism, Socialism and Democracy. The simple characteristic of capitalism is the process of self-destruction. It is a repetitive cycle in which the structure of the economy constantly revolutionizes itself internally, constantly destroying the old one and constantly creating a new one. Schumpeter also calls it "creative destruction". The success of capitalism is due to the active involvement of entrepreneurs in the system, and the innovation mechanism leads to the creation of new enterprises and industries.

Another distinction of the term entrepreneur belongs to Peter Druker, who presents all his evidence in his paper "Innovation and the Entrepreneurial System" (1985). Butler, after analyzing this work came to the conclusion that "the main task in an economy - is to do something different, not to do better something that is already being done". When it comes to innovation, Druker has one message: "wherever you work, you can change the way you do things, and that change could have huge effects". Drucker takes a deeper introspection of this term and starts from the original definition of the economist thinker J.B. Say (1800): 'The entrepreneur moves economic resources from an area of limited productivity to one of high and more profitable productivity'. Being an entrepreneur is thus not a "personality trait, but a quality that can be used in the actions of individuals or institutions", because often an entrepreneur applies what he or she has learned, whether in education, health or some other field, and what they do is not only done correctly, but also because that action results in something different and has a degree of personality. Also, the entrepreneur has the power to "overturn and organize" the economic structure, and "creative destruction" will always confront the unknown, uncertainty, exploitation and how it responds to change.

Another new thinker who identifies other key elements different from those stipulated by Schumpeter is William J. Baumol in his 2010 paper "A Brief History of Innovative Entrepreneurship". First, he distinguishes between entrepreneur and manager. In his view, the manager has qualities such as making the enterprise more efficient, and his work involves "analysis and judgment, but leads to almost nothing new". Baumol makes another distinction, but this time from the perspective of two types of entrepreneurs: the "replicative" and the "innovative" entrepreneur. The "replicative" entrepreneur is the entrepreneur who fits the classic definition, i.e. the person who starts a business, even if he or she does things that others do. The "innovator" entrepreneur is the category honored by both Schumpeter and Baumol, as they are the only ones responsible in an economy for revolutionary development.

Entrepreneurship is the fourth "factor of production" in economic thinking, alongside labor, capital and land. This term has often been ignored because it is the 'product of one mind' and therefore quantified differently. Another reason is that through innovation, entrepreneurs could change the economic circuit, equilibrium and mechanism by creating new industries.

Schumpeter believed that innovation would become routine for entrepreneurs; thus, for Baumol, this criterion means just the opposite. What he is trying to emphasize is that in the early stages of a company/firm's existence, more often than not the decisions made are determined by beliefs as well as irrational periods that lead to ideas that will not produce anything in the future. This is why the fruits of the future are often categorized to small businesses rather than large ones, because the vision of their ideas are more marketable, being intended for public use. The entrepreneur must also be supported by the state, as it helps them to implement their innovative ideas, both passively (through laws, patent projections, etc.) and actively by "funding basic research". Baumol also emphasizes that entrepreneurship is an "important component of the new theory of development", so that in the future we are facing "new heights through the power of ideas".

Another entrepreneurial perspective belongs to Ray Dalio (with his work Principles, 2018), in which he explores the business world from two points of view, namely: the principles of life and the principles of work. Life principles are fundamental guidelines that have shaped his business thinking and actions exclusively transparency, honesty and constant self-evaluation. The Working Principles flow from the way his team and his business apply these principles within Bridgewater Associates, including through an organizational culture based on transparent reasoning and constructive debate.

The entrepreneur is the most complex character in the economic sphere. He is a collection of elements that serve the mass use and exploitation of ideas by the public. Not only must he take a multitude of risks (economic, financial, solvency/bankruptcy), but he must also be discerning that what he produces on the market is feasible and meets the needs of his customers. The entrepreneurial quality is also known by the concept of entrepreneur, which is similar to the entrepreneur of today. This value first appeared in France (18th century) and was studied by the economist Richard Cantillon when he associated economic risk-taking with entrepreneurship. The Industrial Revolution, meanwhile, has a special place in England because it gave entrepreneurs new opportunities to capitalize on ideas and resource potential

2 CHAPTER CHARACTERISTICS OF THE ENTREPRENEUR

Market opportunities are the essential characteristic of an entrepreneur, which is why entrepreneurship is also broadly defined as "the search for opportunities beyond currently existing resources". Entrepreneurs identify and develop them to showcase their work.

An entrepreneur has a number of characteristics, such as: curiosity, willingness to experiment, adaptability, determination, decisiveness, determination, self-awareness, risk tolerance, comfort in the face of failure, persistence, innovative thinking, long-term focus. Entrepreneurship is the main source of today's economic, technological and employment growth, promoting product and service quality, innovation and economic flexibility. This is why it needs to be innovative and identify the necessary needs of the present.

Another highlight can be found in the book "A Practical Guide for Entrepreneurs", where the characteristics of the standard entrepreneur are appreciated. According to this guide can be mentioned: labor-intensive, pursuit of economic success, responsibility, risk-taking, limitation of employee benefits, adaptability to change, business success. Also business experience, honesty, decisiveness, firmness in decision making and links with other partners can be distinguished.

Over time, several characteristics of the entrepreneur have been analyzed. Those that have a prestigious significance in entrepreneurship are the following: Determination and persistence (an important element because the entrepreneur through determination and persistence can achieve a shield against obstacles and risks that can intervene in a business); desire towards success (entrepreneurs analyze an opportunity, examine the chance they can get and how they can get additional profit, have the ability to manage risks to move forward) exploitation of opinions (consumer opinions are important because entrepreneurs can learn from mistakes and experiences they have had previously); proactivity and commitment (entrepreneurs have always been put in difficult situations that could size the success of a business, but through their skills they have managed to turn them into a real advantage to maximize profit, that's why they are considered independent and dynamic beings); self-confidence and posi positivism (self-confidence and positivism refers to the confidence an entrepreneur can develop after enduring failure while becoming a role model for others); vision realization (many entrepreneurs know their limits and have a clear vision of their own business they want to achieve; e.g. Ray Dalio, with his capital market skills, wanted his own firm to advise businesses that preferred to make a profit and prevent risks that could disrupt an entrepreneurial activity, which it did).

The entrepreneur is our creative personality - always at its best when facing the unknown, anticipating the future, creating probabilities out of possibilities, turning chaos into harmony. The entrepreneur is the main character and a symbol of the market economy. Its contribution to society and the substantial role it plays is manifested in its qualitative aspect, which will reach its peak, as many specialists say, in the 21st century, when it will undergo many mutations, hard to imagine today. Again, many institutions and universities are exploring the business world, forming various competitions to generate new business opportunities and business theories

In this case, decision-makers can submit themselves to various programs to support integration/reintegration into the labor market (young people, unemployed) within the European Union. These programs must provide awareness-raising and information, the role that an economic operator must play in the development of its own sector.

This area represents a good solution to stagnating unemployment and overcoming the crisis. It must be supported, first and foremost, by the Romanian state, right from primary school, because financial and entrepreneurial education builds skills which are beneficial for the community. We also need to take into account each country's policy in this area, regional development characteristics and objectives.

3 CHAPTER THE RISKS FOR AN ENTREPRENEUR

Peter Druker argued that risk or the myth of risk arises from the simple fact that the existing entrepreneur does not fully exploit market opportunities. The entrepreneur is risky, he notes, if: "he violates elementary and well-known rules", so that an entrepreneurial activity does not become risky when it is carried out "systematically, organized and well thought out".

Often, at the enterprise level, risk is associated with the risk taken by the entrepreneur. Entrepreneurial risk as an area of analysis is a complex element. The entrepreneur assumes various predispositions to failure from the very beginning of his activity. Risk is the variability of a result obtained or hoped for under the pressure of factors coming from the external environment, materialized in a potential damage to which the assets and/or the activity is exposed. There is a convergence of opinion among those who study economics and, in particular, those who work in this field, that risk in business is normal. It is a natural and inevitable part of doing business. Its disappearance creates confusion, inefficiency and leads to unnatural business behavior, as seen in totalitarian systems. Back then, risk was reduced, often even disappearing, because the economy was run through administrative command levers.

It is also a risk for the entrepreneur when dealing with human capital. Gary Baker points out in "Human Capital" (1964) that education, but especially the accumulation of knowledge, produces an educated society, the end product being the development of the mass economy. Baker also points out that although the experience of school graduates is partly non-existent, they are an important accumulation in the context of development because they are knowledge-based, practical and, most importantly, they can "analyze problems". This is the distinction between an educated or college-educated employee and an uneducated one.

It is also difficult to identify the problems a business often faces. It is important to identify them and not tolerate them. Each problem identified is an opportunity to improve the mechanism. Identifying problems and intolerance of them is one of the most important and most unpleasant things entrepreneurs can do. An important role in identifying the risks and problems facing a business is to know the break-even point. According to economist Josh Kaufman, the break-even point is the point at which total revenues equal total expenses of the business and is the point at which the business starts to create value at the expense of consumption. However, risk can be imminent when we have the knowledge to master it. This is why an entrepreneur needs to know and quantify an investment at the right time. As Druker pointed out, every activity or action must be done "systematically, organized and well thought out", that's how we will succeed as entrepreneurs.

Although being an entrepreneur means taking risks, there are also positive aspects to being an entrepreneur, as follows:
1. Time control (an entrepreneur can manage their time according to the type of business);
2. Fulfillment (a successful entrepreneur is fulfilled and stimulated by the work they do because they are passionate about their business);
3. Creation/ownership (an entrepreneur's goal is to create a business that will bring in a steady stream of

income);
4. Control over remuneration (an entrepreneur chooses how and when to be paid, whether by salary, tariff wage, dividend, commission);
5. Control over working conditions (an entrepreneur builds a working environment in which they can implement their visions).

Thus, an entrepreneur has the power to manage his or her own time for the type of business he or she owns. Also, an entrepreneur is stimulated by the work he or she puts in, which involves a high degree of fulfillment, in order to bring in continuous streams of income. Another important aspect would be that an entrepreneur has the ability to manage their own paycheck and that they build their own community by emphasizing their important values.

4 CHAPTER ENTREPRENEURIAL STRATEGIES

Entrepreneurial strategies are a set of well-thought-out directions and action plans designed to achieve business success. In doing so, entrepreneurs not only respond to essential needs in the marketplace, but envision and shape the future. In the amplified context of strategies we will consider a first topic for discussion, namely what the strategic goal entails from Michael E. Gerber's perspective.

The strategic objective is a very clear statement of what the built business must ultimately do in order to achieve its main goal (...) The strategic objective is not a business plan. It is a product of the life plan, just like the strategy and the business plan.

Generically, we could say that the strategic objective is a clear and concise statement of what a company or entity aims to achieve in the long term in order to achieve its vision and mission. They typically provide direction and guidance to the organization to guide itself in decision-making and allocate resources effectively. The strategic objective must be characterized by a series of elements such as: specificity, measurability, tangibility, relevance, limited time.

As for the specificity of the strategic objective, it must be as clear and well-defined as possible, in order to be easy to understand and follow. It is important to evaluate the achievement of the objective, therefore they must be measurable. At the same time, the objectives must be real and feasible, in accordance with the resources and environmental conditions available. The objectives must be relevant to the company's mission and vision. They contribute to the achievement of the overall strategic direction. Setting a deadline adds an element of clarity by specifying the time to achieve the goal. That is why "he who does not know his objectives well does not know how to oppose the enemy" (in our case competition), thus "the smallest certainly cannot be measured with the great, nor the weak with the strong or the few with the crowd" as described by Sun Tzu in his treatise on strategy, political thought and intelligence training.

At the level of a company, an organization must also be carried out at the same time in order to develop more intelligently, so consequently an organizational strategy. Michael E. Gerber also addresses such a context and states the following: "We knew that the organizational evolution reflected in the organizational chart can have a more profound impact on a small company than any single step of business development. Most companies are organized around personalities rather than functions".

Also within a company we can also talk about marketing strategies, for employees, management, etc., but also what the company comes up with, so that element of novelty. It can be said that based on the strategies applied, the company develops something new, a new distribution, a new service to attract customers and to choose their loyalty. Josh Kaufman describes in his work: "***Novelty*** —the presence of new sensory data — is critical if you want to attract or maintain attention for a longer period of time. One of the reasons people can focus for hours on video games or when browsing the internet is novelty – every viral clip, blog post, Facebook update, tweet or news reengages your ability to pay attention." So, a company must update its strategies **and** always come up with something new that keeps the continuity of customers.

5 CHAPTER STIMULATING ENTREPRENEURSHIP

Stimulating entrepreneurship is essential for the economic and social development of a country. It can lead to job creation, innovation and increased economic competitiveness. Here are some detailed strategies through which entrepreneurship can be stimulated:

1. **Education and Training:**

a. Introduction of entrepreneurship education in schools: Starting from the secondary school cycle, students should be exposed to basic concepts of entrepreneurship. This can include courses in economics, management, and case studies of successful businesses.
b. Specialized university programs: Universities should offer bachelor's and master's degree programs in entrepreneurship, including practical courses, mentorship, and access to business networks.
c. Courses and workshops: Non-governmental organizations and private companies can organize courses and workshops to learn the skills needed to start and run a business.

2. **Access to Financing:**

a. Government funds and grants: Governments can create specialized funds and grant programs for start-ups and small and medium-sized enterprises (SMEs).
b. Improving access to credit: Financial institutions should develop flexible and affordable lending products for entrepreneurs, such as micro-loans and low-interest long-term loans.
c. Venture capital investments and angel investors: Encouraging private investment through tax incentives and creating networks of investors interested in financing innovative start-ups.

3. **Infrastructure and Support:**

a. Incubators and accelerators: Creation of centers that provide logistical support, mentoring, and access to business networks for start-ups, allowing them to grow and develop faster.
b. Special Economic Zones: Designation of special economic zones with favorable tax facilities and regulations to attract investment and stimulate entrepreneurial development.
c. Access to technology: Ensuring access to digital infrastructure, such as high-speed internet and e-commerce platforms, is essential for modern entrepreneurs.

4. **Favorable Regulations:**

a. Simplifying the procedures for setting up a business: Reducing the bureaucracy and costs associated with setting up and running a business can encourage more people to become entrepreneurs.
b. Attractive tax regulations: Implementation of favorable tax regimes for start-ups and SMEs, including tax reductions and tax exemptions for the first years of activity.
c. Intellectual property protection: Improving intellectual property protection legislation to encourage innovation and protect entrepreneurs' inventions and ideas.

5. Culture and Attitude:

a. Promoting entrepreneurial culture: Awareness campaigns and promoting local entrepreneurial successes can inspire and motivate other potential entrepreneurs.
b. Community support: Local communities and business networks can play a crucial role in supporting entrepreneurs by providing advice, mentoring, and access to resources.
c. Tolerance for failure: Creating a culture that accepts failure as part of the learning and growth process can encourage more people to take the risk of starting a business.

6. Partnerships and Collaborations:

a. Collaboration with the private sector: Partnerships between governments, universities and the private sector can facilitate the transfer of knowledge and resources to entrepreneurs.
b. International collaborations: Exchange programs and international collaborations can bring new ideas and successful practices, giving entrepreneurs access to global markets and resources.

7. Support for under-represented groups:

a. Specific programs for women entrepreneurs: Creating support and funding programs dedicated to women entrepreneurs can help increase diversity and inclusion in the business environment.
b. Supporting entrepreneurship in rural areas: Developing specific programmes to support entrepreneurs in rural areas, including access to finance and training.
c. Integration of minorities: Ensuring that ethnic minorities and other underrepresented groups have equal access to entrepreneurial opportunities and necessary resources.

In conclusion, fostering entrepreneurship requires a holistic approach, including education, financing, infrastructure, favorable regulations, supportive culture, partnerships, and support for underrepresented groups. Implementing these strategies can create an environment conducive to business development and contribute to long-term economic and social prosperity.

6 CHAPTER INVOLVEMENT OF TIMERS IN ENTREPRENEURSHIP ACTIVITIES

Stimulating young people to participate in entrepreneurship activities is vital for the economic and social development of a country. This can be achieved through a series of well-thought-out strategies that involve education, access to resources, community support, and favorable regulations. In the following, I will describe in detail some methods for involving young people in the business environment.

1. **Education and Training**

a. **Introducing entrepreneurship courses in schools:** Entrepreneurship education needs to start early. Integrating entrepreneurship courses into the school curriculum, starting with secondary school and continuing in high school, can be of great help. Students can learn through interactive methods such as role-plays, group projects, and case studies, which can give them a practical understanding of how businesses work.
b. **Dedicated university programs:** Universities should offer courses and degree programs focused on entrepreneurship. These can include idea competitions and hackathons that stimulate creativity and innovation. Universities can also collaborate with successful entrepreneurs to provide students with mentors to guide them.
c. **Workshops and seminars:** Workshops and seminars on various topics related to entrepreneurship, organized by schools, universities and non-profit organizations, can provide young people with the necessary knowledge and skills. Inviting successful entrepreneurs to share their experiences can inspire and motivate young people.

2. **Access to Resources and Funding**

a. **Grants and scholarships:**

Offering specific grants and scholarships for young entrepreneurs can facilitate the launch of new businesses. Special investment funds for youth-led start-ups can attract innovative ideas and support their development.

b. **Access to incubators and accelerators:**

The establishment of incubators and accelerators that provide logistical support, mentoring and funding is essential. These centers can provide young entrepreneurs with workspaces, technical resources and networking opportunities.

c. Partnerships with the private sector:

Working with companies to offer internships and mentoring programs for young people is crucial. Also, incentivizing companies to invest in start-ups through tax benefits can attract additional investment.

3. Creating a Supportive Environment

a. Simplifying regulations:

Cutting red tape and simplifying business start-up procedures are key to encouraging young people to become entrepreneurs. Implementing favorable tax regimes for young entrepreneurs can reduce the initial financial burden.

b. Promoting entrepreneurial culture:

Awareness campaigns and promoting successful examples among young people can encourage other young people to follow their entrepreneurial dreams. Organizing events, fairs and conferences dedicated to youth entrepreneurship can create a platform for exposure and recognition.

d. Community support:

Creating support networks and discussion groups for young entrepreneurs can provide a framework in which they can share their experiences and support each other. Local communities play an important role in supporting entrepreneurial initiatives.

4. Developing personal skills

a. Skills development programs:

Organizing courses and workshops to develop essential skills, such as leadership, time management, and effective communication, is vital. They can be offered by schools, universities, and non-profit organizations.

b. Encouraging innovation and creativity:

Projects and competitions that stimulate innovative and creative thinking are important for the development of business ideas. Support for prototype development and idea testing can turn concepts into reality.

c. Developing a risk-taking mindset:

Education on the importance of risk-taking and learning from failures is crucial. Creating an environment where failure is perceived as a learning opportunity and not as an obstacle can encourage more young people to take entrepreneurial risks.

5. Networking and Mentoring

a. Mentoring program:

Establishing mentoring programs in which experienced entrepreneurs guide young people in their endeavors is essential. These programs can provide practical advice and moral support.

b. Networking networks:

Organsin networking events to enable young people to create professional relationships and find business partners is vital. Online networking and collaboration platforms for young entrepreneurs can make it easier to connect and exchange ideas.

c. International collaborations:

Exchange programmers and international collaborations can expose young people to successful ideas and practices from other countries. Access to global markets through international partnerships can open up new business opportunities.

6. Support for Diverse Youth Groups

a. Inclusion and diversity:

Programmes dedicated to young people from disadvantaged backgrounds, ethnic minorities or other underrepresented groups can ensure that all young people have access to entrepreneurial resources and opportunities.

b. Support for rural youth:

Targeted initiatives for rural youth, including access to vocational training and finance, can reduce disparities and encourage the development of entrepreneurship in these areas.

7. Recognizing and Rewarding Success

a. Awards and recognition:
Organizing competitions and awarding prizes for successful ideas and businesses can motivate young people to participate in entrepreneurial activities. Public recognition of young entrepreneurs' achievements through the media and other channels can provide visibility and encouragement.

b. Start-up of the year programmes:
Initiatives that recognize and reward the most innovative and successful youth-led start-ups annually can create a culture of entrepreneurial excellence and ambition.

By implementing these strategies, we can create a favorable environment for young entrepreneurs, providing them with the necessary resources and support to turn their ideas into reality and contribute to the economic and social development of society.

7 CHAPTER PROBLEMS FACED BY ENTREPRENEURSHIP

Entrepreneurship is a field full of challenges and opportunities, involving starting, growing and running your own business. While many success stories are often highlighted in the media, the reality is that entrepreneurship comes with a myriad of problems that founders must overcome to succeed. This description will explore in detail some of the main issues facing entrepreneurs in today's business world.

I. Access to finance

One of the biggest challenges for entrepreneurs is raising the capital needed to start and grow a business. For start-ups in particular, access to finance can be difficult as investors and banks are often reluctant to invest in start-ups without a strong track record. Entrepreneurs need to explore various sources of funding, including venture capital, bank loans, crowdfunding and government grants. However, each of these options comes with its own requirements and risks, making access to finance a complex and time-consuming task.

II. Cash flow management

Cash flow management is essential for the survival of a business, but it is also one of the most common problems entrepreneurs face. Many entrepreneurs underestimate operating costs and overestimate revenues, which can lead to cash flow problems. It is vital that contractors keep accurate records of cash inflows and outflows and plan in advance for periods of declining revenues. It is also important to negotiate favorable payment terms with suppliers and improve debt collection policies.

III. Intense Competition

Whatever the industry, competition is a major challenge for entrepreneurs. Markets are often saturated with existing players with superior resources and experience. To differentiate themselves, entrepreneurs need to constantly innovate and offer unique products or services that address unmet market needs. It is also essential to develop a strong marketing strategy and build a recognizable and trusted brand.

IV. Regulatory Changes and Red Tape

Government regulations and red tape can be significant obstacles for entrepreneurs. Each industry has its own regulations and these can vary significantly from region to region. Entrepreneurs need to be aware of all legal requirements and ensure their business is compliant. Failure to comply with regulations can lead to costly fines and other legal penalties. In addition, the process of registering a business and obtaining the necessary licenses can be lengthy and complicated, adding an extra layer of difficulty in launching a business.

V. Time Management

Entrepreneurs must juggle numerous responsibilities, from product and service development to marketing, sales, finance and human resources. Effective time management is essential to business success. Many entrepreneurs face burnout due to the high workload and stress associated with running a business. It's important to learn to prioritize tasks, delegate responsibilities when possible, and set aside time for rest and recovery.

VI. Attracting and retaining talent

Another major issue for entrepreneurs is attracting and retaining talented employees. Large companies have the resources to offer competitive salaries and extensive benefits, making them more attractive to candidates. Entrepreneurs must find ways to attract talent by providing a dynamic work environment, opportunities for professional growth and a positive organizational culture. It is also essential to invest in employee development and provide recognition and rewards for their performance.

VII. Innovation and adaptability

In an ever-changing world, innovation and adaptability are crucial to the long-term success of a business. Technology is evolving rapidly and consumer preferences are constantly changing. Entrepreneurs must be willing to adapt their business strategy and innovate their products and services to stay relevant in the marketplace. This may involve significant investment in research and development as well as openness to customer feedback and market trends.

VIII. Building and maintaining reputation

A business's reputation is key to attracting and retaining customers. In the digital age, online reviews and social media play a crucial role in shaping public perception. Entrepreneurs must actively manage their business' online presence, respond quickly and professionally to negative feedback and engage in ethical and transparent business practices. A solid reputation can build trust and loyalty, while a negative one can lead to significant losses.

IX. Managing risk and uncertainty

Entrepreneurship involves taking risks and navigating uncertainty. Economic, political or technological changes can have a major impact on the business. It is essential that entrepreneurs develop risk management strategies, diversify their sources of income and build up financial reserves to cope with potential crises. The ability to assess risks and make informed decisions is an essential skill for any successful entrepreneur.

X. Developing relationships and networks

Building a strong network of contacts and relationships is vital to entrepreneurial success. Entrepreneurs must invest time and effort in developing relationships with customers, suppliers, investors and other business partners. Attending networking events, joining professional organizations and working with mentors can provide valuable support and opportunities. A strong network can facilitate access to resources, information and support, contributing to business growth and development.

Entrepreneurship is a challenging journey, but it is also full of unique opportunities. Success in business requires not only an innovative idea, but also the ability to overcome the many problems along the way. From accessing finance and managing cash flow, to attracting talent and adapting to change, entrepreneurs must be prepared to meet these challenges with resilience, creativity and determination. Ultimately, the ability to navigate and learn from these difficulties can turn challenges into opportunities for growth and success.

8 CHAPTER SOLUTIONS RELATED TO THE PROBLEMS ANALYZED IN THE PREVIOUS CHAPTER

Entrepreneurship involves navigating a challenging and uncertain landscape. However, many of the common problems can be prevented or managed effectively through well thought out and implemented strategies. This description will explore ways in which entrepreneurs can prevent the main problems encountered in running a business.

1. Access to Finance

To prevent difficulties accessing finance, entrepreneurs need to prepare thoroughly before seeking capital. It is essential to develop a solid and detailed business plan that outlines growth potential and demonstrates the viability of the business. They should also explore all available options such as venture capital, bank loans, crowdfunding and government grants. Establishing a good financial track record and maintaining strong relationships with banks and investors can make it easier to access funding in the future.

2. Cash Flow Management

To avoid cash flow problems, entrepreneurs should implement a rigorous cash monitoring and management system. It is important to make realistic financial projections and regularly review the budget to anticipate periods of shortfalls. Negotiating longer payment terms with suppliers and encouraging customers to pay quickly through discount offers can improve cash flow. Contractors should also build up financial reserves to cope with unexpected difficulties.

3. Intense Competition

To differentiate themselves in a competitive market, entrepreneurs must constantly innovate and offer unique products or services. Conducting a detailed market analysis to identify unmet customer needs can help develop distinctive offerings. A well-defined marketing strategy and building a strong brand are crucial. Investments in technology and ongoing team training can ensure adaptability and sustainable competitive advantage.

4. Regulatory Changes and Red Tape

To successfully navigate regulations and red tape, entrepreneurs must be proactive in informing and complying with legal requirements. Hiring legal counsel or a compliance specialist can be of great help. It is also useful to get involved in business associations and entrepreneur networks that can provide support and information about legislative changes. Meticulous planning and proper documentation can prevent delays and legal complications.

5. Time Management

Effective time management can be achieved by prioritizing tasks and delegating responsibilities. Entrepreneurs must learn to say "no" to activities that do not add value to the business and focus on strategic objectives. Using time management tools such as digital calendars and productivity apps can improve organization and efficiency. Establishing regular routines and rest periods is essential to prevent burnout.

6. Attracting and Retaining Talent

To attract and retain talent, entrepreneurs need to create an attractive and motivating work environment. Offering competitive salaries and attractive benefits is important, but not enough. Professional development opportunities, recognition of merit and a positive organizational culture are essential. Investing in employee training and development and involving employees in decision-making can increase loyalty and job satisfaction.

7. Innovation and Adaptability

Entrepreneurs need to cultivate a culture of innovation and adaptability within their organization. This involves encouraging employees to come up with new ideas and experiment. Constantly monitoring market trends and customer feedback can help identify opportunities for innovation. Investment in technology and continuous training are also crucial to maintain competitiveness. Flexibility and openness to change must be built into the organization's DNA.

8. Creating and Maintaining Reputation

To create and maintain a positive reputation, entrepreneurs must engage in ethical and transparent business practices. Actively managing their online presence and responding quickly and professionally to customer feedback are essential. Providing quality service and delivering on promises are fundamental to building trust. In addition, participating in corporate social responsibility activities can improve public perception and strengthen the reputation of the business.

9. Managing Risk and Uncertainty

Entrepreneurs must develop sound risk management strategies to navigate through uncertainty. This involves identifying and assessing potential risks and implementing mitigation measures. Diversifying income sources and building financial reserves can provide a safety net in the event of crises. Regular assessment of the business environment and adjusting plans in response to economic, political or technological changes are essential to maintain stability.

10. Developing Relationships and Networking

Building a solid network of contacts can be facilitated by attending networking events and joining professional organizations. Entrepreneurs should invest time and effort in developing relationships with customers, suppliers, investors and other business partners. Working with mentors and industry experts can provide valuable insights and support in managing challenges. A well-maintained network can open up new opportunities and facilitate access to critical resources and information.

Preventing problems in entrepreneurship requires a combination of strategic planning, adaptability and effective resource management. By implementing sound and proactive practices, entrepreneurs can successfully navigate challenges and ensure the growth and sustainability of their business. Ultimately, success in entrepreneurship depends on the ability to learn from experiences, constantly innovate and maintain a strong commitment to excellence and integrity.

ABOUT THE AUTHOR

The author who reported this information is a graduate of the Faculty of Economics, Administration and Business, which allowed to highlight some essential information of today's business. Entrepreneurship or business in general is influenced by various problems, and they can be mastered through an analysis of management, financial resources, etc., thus, this paper relates and highlights these problems as well as their prevention.

www.ingramcontent.com/pod-product-compliance
Lightning Source LLC
Chambersburg PA
CBHW082242220526
45479CB00005B/1318